# LEGENDS OF WARFARE
### AVIATION

# B-58 Hustler

## Convair's Cold War Mach 2 Bomber

## DAVID DOYLE

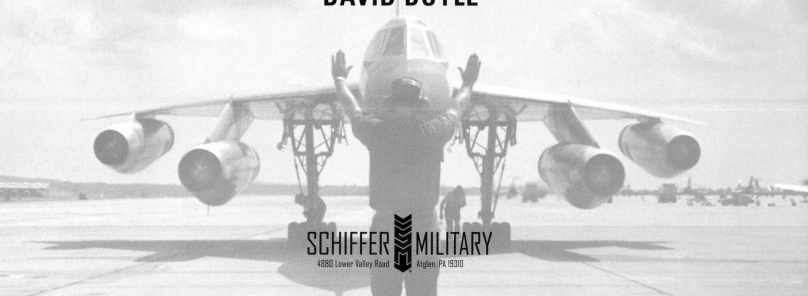

SCHIFFER MILITARY
4880 Lower Valley Road    Atglen, PA 19310

Designed by Justin Watkinson
Type set in Impact/Minion Pro/Univers LT Std

ISBN: 978-0-7643-6131-9
Printed in China

Published by Schiffer Publishing, Ltd.
4880 Lower Valley Road
Atglen, PA 19310
Phone: (610) 593-1777; Fax: (610) 593-2002
E-mail: Info@schifferbooks.com
www.schifferbooks.com

For our complete selection of fine books on this and related subjects, please visit our website at www.schifferbooks.com. You may also write for a free catalog.

Schiffer Publishing's titles are available at special discounts for bulk purchases for sales promotions or premiums. Special editions, including personalized covers, corporate imprints, and excerpts, can be created in large quantities for special needs. For more information, contact the publisher.

We are always looking for people to write books on new and related subjects. If you have an idea for a book, please contact us at proposals@schifferbooks.com.

# Acknowledgments

I have been blessed with the generous help of many friends and colleagues when preparing this manuscript. Truly, this book would not have been possible without their collective assistance. Tom Kailbourn, Stan Piet, Scott Taylor, Dana Bell, the San Diego Air and Space Museum, the American Aviation Historical Society, and especially Brett Stolle and the staff at the National Museum of the United States Air Force all gave of their time without hesitation. My lovely and dear wife, Denise, scanned photos, proofread manuscripts, and was my personal cheerleader throughout the difficult parts of this project, and without her unflagging support this could not have been completed.

# Contents

# Introduction

The Convair B-58 Hustler was the world's first production supersonic bomber, and today, more than sixty years after its first flight, it remains one of only a handful of bombers worldwide to achieve that milestone.

The genesis for what became the B-58 can found in the second Generalized Bomber Study (GEBO II), a project initiated by the Air Force Air Research and Development Command in February 1949. This set in motion the US effort to create a supersonic bomber. Initially, much of this effort was centered on a parasitic aircraft, which would be carried by larger aircraft to a launch point near the target.

By January 1951, the program had evolved such that the bomber would no longer be a parasite but have a long-range capability of its own, enhanced by air-to-air refueling. Various designs were proposed by the nation's aviation firms, with Convair favoring the delta wing, a style the company had some experience with through its previous XF-92 program.

On January 26, 1951, Convair submitted its "Proposal for Development and Manufacture of Long Range Bomber/Reconnaissance Airplane" to the Air Material Command (AMC). AMC designated the type MX-1626 on February 17, 1951.

The Convair design faced competition from Boeing, whose MX-1712 represented the Seattle company's attempt at achieving the same goal. However, on November 18, 1952, Gen. Hoyt S. Vandenberg announced that the Convair offering had won the design competition. Despite Convair having been declared the winner, there was still considerable work to be done on the design. From 1950 through 1954, assorted models were tested both in wind tunnels and by having rockets carry them aloft and releasing them.

On December 2, 1952, Maj. Gen. Donald Putt, chief of the Experimental Bombardment Aircraft Branch, wrote to Convair president J. T. McNarney, stating that their supersonic bomber would be designated the B-58.

By mid-April 1952, the project had been redesignated MX-1964. Along the way the fuselage of the Convair design was modified to incorporate the "area rule" with its characteristic Coke bottle shape. This design feature narrows the fuselage of the aircraft in the area where wings join and, to a lesser extent, in the vicinity of the cockpit, significantly reducing drag in the high-subsonic-speed range.

It was determined that the aircraft would use the X-24A engine then under development by General Electric. As the actual contract was being negotiated, it was stipulated that delays in development of the X-24A were not to delay the B-58 program, and if necessary the Pratt & Whitney J57 would be used as an alternate pending refinement of the X-24A.

Finally, on February 12, 1953, a contract was signed between the Air Force and Convair for the manufacture of the B-58. It would be March before firm specifications were set out and the creation of a full-scale mockup could begin. It would take another year and several variations of the mockup before the B-58 was fully formed.

Although Convair developed several conceptual delta-wing bomber concepts following World War II, a direct antecedent of the B-58 Hustler was the Convair MX-1626, a 1951 design for a long-range supersonic reconnaissance bomber. *American Aviation Historical Society*

In November 1952, Convair won a contest with Boeing to design an advanced supersonic bomber, designated the MX-1964. Not long after that, the design was redesignated the B-58. This drawing features a conceptual powered weapons pod. *American Aviation Historical Society*

The aircraft that would become the Convair B-58 underwent several changes during its design phase. In this conceptual drawing, the jet engines are mounted in twin pods. The large weapons pod underneath the fuselage would become a key component of the B-58. *American Aviation Historical Society*

In a 1953 conceptual drawing, the B-58 has a twin-engine pod under each wing, sometimes called a "Siamese twin" configuration. Aside from the twin-jet-pod arrangement, the design is quite similar to that of the production B-58. *American Aviation Historical Society*

Convair completed this mockup of the MX-1984 in late 1952. From then through much of 1953, the design featured a droppable weapon pod called the lower component, tightly fitted to the underside of the fuselage (the upper component).

The mockup representing the final design of the B-58 is on the floor of US Air Force Plant 4, Fort Worth, Texas, where Convair produced the Hustlers, around August 1954. The full-scale mockup exhibited key characteristics of the yet-to-come production planes, including the pointed nose; the pilot's wraparound windscreen; the tapered, "Coke bottle" fuselage section between the delta wings, based on the then-new area rule theory; the cambered leading edges of the wings; the four separate, close-fitting underwing engine nacelles; and the droppable weapons pod under the belly.

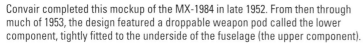

## Specifications

| | |
|---|---|
| Crew: | 3: pilot; observer (navigator, radar operator, bombardier); defense systems operator (DSO; electronic countermeasures operator and pilot assistant) |
| Length: | 96 ft., 10 in. |
| Wingspan: | 56 ft., 9 in. |
| Height: | 29 ft., 11 in. |
| Wing area: | 1,542 ft.² |
| Empty weight: | 55,560 lbs. |
| Loaded weight: | 67,871 lbs. |
| Max. takeoff weight: | 176,890 lbs. |
| Power plant: | 4 × General Electric J79-GE-5A turbojet Dry thrust: 10,400 lbs.-f dry thrust each Thrust with afterburner: 15,600 lbs.-f each |

## Performance

| | |
|---|---|
| Maximum speed: | Mach 2.0 (1,319 mph) at 40,000 ft. |
| Cruise speed: | 610 mph |
| Combat radius: | 1,740 miles |
| Ferry range: | 4,700 miles |
| Service ceiling: | 63,400 ft. |
| Rate of climb: | 17,400 ft./min. at gross weight |
| Thrust/weight: | 0.919 lbs.-f |

## Armament

| | |
|---|---|
| Guns: | 1 × 20 mm T171 cannon |
| Bombs: | 4 × B43 or B61 nuclear bombs; maximum weapons load was 19,450 lbs. Weapons in the pod included a W39Y1-1 thermonuclear warhead in the MB-1 pod or a Mk. 53 thermonuclear warhead in the upper part of the two-component pod |

## Serial numbers

| | |
|---|---|
| 55-660 through 55-1023 | YB/RB-58A |
| 59-2428 through 59-2463 | B-58A |
| 60-1110 through 60-2080 | B-58A |

The first of two prototypes, YB/RB-58A-1-CF, serial number 55-0660, was covered with nylon to mask its shape for security purposes while being transferred to the final assembly area. Engine nacelles were yet to be mounted under the wings, and other components remained to be installed. *American Aviation Historical Society*

Unlike most previous US bombers, the Hustler did not have an XB variant. Rather, it went from drawing board to YB—or service test—aircraft. The schedule set forth in January 1953 called for the first aircraft to be completed in January 1956. The first thirty, or the YB series, would be divided into two groups. The first eighteen aircraft would be powered by the Pratt & Whitney J57-P-15 engines. The next twelve would get early trial versions of the J79-GE-1 engines, rated at only fifty hours. The J79 was the production version of the previously mentioned X-24A engine. Subsequent aircraft beyond the first thirty, or in other words, the full-production B-58s, would be powered by standard production J79s, rated at 150 hours.

After a thorough review of the mockup and plans, on December 4, 1953, the Wright Air Development Center approved fabrication of the first aircraft to begin, starting with the front wing spar, secondary wing spar, and chordwise bulkheads.

In March 1954 the schedule was significantly revised in hopes of having a more fully refined aircraft reach operational squadrons. As a result of the March revisions, the first nine aircraft, which were to be powered by the J57-P-15, were to be designated YB-58. Aircraft 10 through 30 were to be equipped with full-production J79 engines. Starting with the thirteenth aircraft, to be delivered December 1958–January 1959, the aircraft were to be delivered to the Strategic Air Command (SAC). The secretary of the Air Force approved this schedule on April 30, 1954, and released the funds to procure the aircraft.

In May 1954, SAC requested various changes in the design, including, significantly, the placement of the copilot next to rather than behind the pilot. In order to incorporate these changes, Convair pushed the scheduled first flight date back from January 1956 to June 1956.

Further disagreements within the Air Force and between the Air Force and Convair concerning design details continued to push back the targeted first flight date. Many of these stemmed from SAC chief Gen. Curtis LeMay's outright opposition to the aircraft.

In 1956, the name "Hustler," which had unofficially been used by Convair for some time, was officially made the name of the B-58.

On September 1, 1956, the first prototype, serial number 55-660, rolled out of Convair's facility in Fort Worth, Texas. One month later, the aircraft had its first engine run-up tests, firing the J79s in the aircraft for the first time. The many delays in the B-58 program meant that the engines were ready when the airplane was, negating the need to use J57s as planned on the first aircraft.

The first taxi test was held on October 29, and the first flight on Sunday, November 11, 1956.

As planned, the first thirty aircraft were used for testing. The testing phase was somewhat protracted, in part due to the complexity of the aircraft and delays in the refinement of some of its many systems, in particular the navigation system. Plus, the aircraft had to be tested for in-flight refueling, low-altitude penetration and bombing, and high-altitude bombing.

During these tests, aircraft 58-1008 was lost on December 16, 1958, when an electrical failure in flight led to a loss of control. This was the first Hustler lost—unfortunately, there would be twenty-five more, including a total of nine of the service test YB aircraft. All three crew aboard 58-1008 ejected, but pilot Maj. Richard Smith's parachute did not open. Navigator Lt. Col. George Gradel and DSO Capt. Daniel Holland made successful ejections and survived. However, having ejected at 650 mph, they were severely battered by the airstream, including many broken limbs. This pointed to the need for an improved ejection system.

The first prototype YB/RB-58A is parked on a hardstand. All three of the cabin hatch doors are in the open positions. From front to rear, the positions were for the pilot, the bombardier/navigator, and the defense systems operator (DSO). The two latter crewmen had a small window to each side of their cabins. The hatch and cabin interiors were white. *National Museum of the United States Air Force*

Convair YB/RB-58A, serial number 55-0660, assumes a nose-high attitude as it takes off, with the main landing-gear wheels, eight per side, still firmly in contact with the runway. This aircraft made its first flight on November 11, 1956, from Carswell Air Force Base, near the Convair plant. That flight also marked the public debut of the Hustler. *American Aviation Historical Society*

The first YB/RB-58A is viewed from below during flight, with the weapons pod not installed, thus permitting an unimpeded view of the belly of the fuselage. Note the many tones of the bare-metal panels on the wings and the engine nacelles. *National Archives*

Three of the men closely associated with the B-58 program pose for their photo in front of the first YB/RB-58A. *Left to right*, they are J. T. Cosby, manager of the Convair B-58 program; Vincent Dolson, who directed the construction program for the first thirteen YB-58As; and August Esenwein, manager of Convair's Fort Worth factory. *National Museum of the United States Air Force*

In a right-side view of the number one YB/RB-58A, there are what appear to be at first glance smudges on the nose and main landing-gear tires. These were squares of white paint that were applied to the tires for reference markings prior to motion pictures being taken of the tires during landings and takeoffs, in order to assess their performance. *National Museum of the United States Air Force*

The first YB/RB-58A received a new paint scheme after its early test flights, with pointed red-and-white designs on the forward fuselage, wingtips, and vertical tail giving the impression of forward motion. The weapons pod was painted red, with a wide black band visible on the side. A black antiglare panel was painted to the front of the windscreen. *Stan Piet collection*

Various weapons pods were tested on the YB/RB-58As; the second prototype, serial number 55-661, was the first Hustler to make a test flight carrying a weapons pod. The nose landing-gear strut was of complex design, featuring a strut with a hinge in the middle so that the gear could clear the nose of the weapons pod. *National Archives*

At Run Station No. 2 at the Convair factory at Fort Worth, on December 27, 1956, engine tests are being conducted on YB/RB-58A, serial number 55-0660. By now, the interiors of the crew hatch doors had dark-colored linings.

In a photo likely taken on the same date as the preceding two photos, the first YB/RB-58A is viewed from the left rear during preparations for engine tests in Run Station No. 2 at the Convair plant in Fort Worth. Near the top of the dorsal fin is a boom, evidently a data-link antenna that sometimes was installed on test aircraft.

Convair YB/RB-58A, serial number 55-0660, is viewed from ground level at Run Station No. 2 on December 27, 1956. A cover with multicolored caution pennants hanging from it has been installed over the nose boom.

This is the third Hustler built, YB/RB-58A serial number 55-0662, shown wearing the early red, white, and polished aluminum paint scheme. *American Aviation Historical Society*

The second prototype Hustler was YB/RB-58A, serial number 55-0661. At the time the photo was taken, this plane had paintwork that was similar to one of the early paint schemes of the first YB/RB-58A, with red areas with white arrowhead-like overlays. White reference marks are on the tires. For taxiing tests, screen-type covers are installed over the engine intakes to prevent them from sucking in foreign objects. *National Museum of the United States Air Force*

To assist the Hustler in slowing down upon landing, a drag chute, also referred to as a deceleration parachute system, was installed at the lower rear of the fuselage. Here, YB/RB-58A comes to a stop upon landing, with chute lines visible to the right. *National Museum of the United States Air Force*

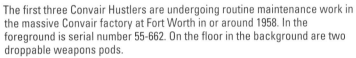

The first three Convair Hustlers are undergoing routine maintenance work in the massive Convair factory at Fort Worth in or around 1958. In the foreground is serial number 55-662. On the floor in the background are two droppable weapons pods.

An early YB/RB-58A with an MB-1 free-fall weapons pod installed is parked in a run station at the Convair plant. The tail number is indistinct, but the last digit appears to be a "7," so this plane may have been serial number 55-667. On the fuselage above the front of the nose-gear bay is the insignia of the B-58 Test Force.

The MB-1 was the type of weapons pod carried by Hustlers during the early part of the flight test program and in the first years of the plane's operational career. As opposed to the rocket-powered weapons pods that would be developed for the B-58, the MB-1 was a free-fall design. The pod was 51 feet long by 5 feet in diameter and had its own built-in pylon. It carried both auxiliary fuel and a W39Y1-1 thermonuclear warhead; when the warhead was not installed, it was necessary to place ballast of matching weight in the pod in order to sustain the B-58's flight characteristics. *American Aviation Historical Society*

Weapons pods were manufactured on the assembly line at Convair's Fort Worth plant along with the B-58s. A completed pod is on the trolley at the center, while other pods are under assembly to the sides and in the background. *San Diego Air and Space Museum*

The fourth YB/RB-58A, serial number 55-663, is parked at a desert airbase. Several civilians are looking on as another civilian is making an adjustment to a connection on the top of an MB-1 droppable weapons pod numbered B-111. A panel has been removed from atop the fuselage between the cockpit and the middle cabin.

Among other achievements, the second YB/RB-58A, serial number 55-661, was the first Hustler to drop a weapons pod during a test flight and the first to complete an in-air refueling. When photographed, the nickname "Mach-in-Boid" had been painted below the windscreen; below the nickname is the B-58 Test Force insignia. *American Aviation Historical Society*

Ladders are set up alongside the cockpit and center cabin of "Mach-in-Boid" at an unidentified airfield in the desert around the late 1950s. This may have been at Edwards Air Force Base, California, where this plane performed low-level ejection-seat tests; on February 28, 1962, this Hustler was the first one to test the ejection of a live human subject. *American Aviation Historical Society*

"Mach-in-Boid," the second YB/RB-58A, is observed from the left side with no weapons pod installed, showing its nickname painted in white letters arranged in a slight curve below the windscreen. *National Archives*

"Mach-in-Boid" is poised on a taxiway at Carswell Air Force Base, Texas, on December 9, 1959. A good view is available of the tail cone that was installed where the tail turret eventually would be located; above the tail cone is a bullet-shaped extension on the lower part of the vertical tail, which will house the radome for the fire-control radar. *National Archives*

During the plane's flight test period, "Mach-in-Boid" is seen from the right front at Carswell Air Force Base, Texas, on December 9, 1959. This plane would be converted to a TB-58A trainer and also would go on to serve with the 305th Bombardment Wing. *National Archives*

Considerable effort and testing went into devising safe methods and equipment for ejecting crewmen from the B-58. Convair designed and produced its own ejection seats, called the SACseat. This high-speed sled, built to resemble the forward fuselage of the Hustler, was used for testing the SACseat at the Naval Ordnance Research Track at China Lake, California, starting in February 1956. *American Aviation Historical Society*

A pack of rocket motors on the rear of the sled have ignited at the beginning of a test run to study the performance of the SACseat at China Lake. *American Aviation Historical Society*

During a test of the SACseat in the test sled at China Lake on August 7, 1958, the unit has just been ejected from the act cabin of the sled. In lieu of a human guinea pig, strapped to the seat was a 200-pound dummy. Tests indicated that the SACseat was not going to give the crewmen of the B-58 sufficient protection, and other means of ejecting crewmen were studied. *National Museum of the United States Air Force*

The answer to the dilemma of providing a sufficiently protective ejection system for the B-58 crewmen was the encapsulated ejection seat developed by Convair and the Stanley Aviation Corporation. The encapsulated ejection seat featured a clamshell door that closed before ejection, to provide the crewman with a pressurized environment and protection from the effects of high-speed ejection at high altitude. One of the encapsulated seats is viewed from the front with the clamshell door open, showing the headrest, harness, cushions, and capsule floor. The pilot's capsule included his control stick on the floor.

A crew capsule is seen from the rear, showing the folded-back clamshell door. The first in-flight ejection test of the crew capsule was made from YB/RB-58A, serial number 55-661, over Edwards Air Force Base in October 1961. Following an ejection test using a live chimpanzee, a subsonic test using a human subject was made on February 28, 1962. For the first supersonic test of the capsule, a small bear was used as the subject!

The escape capsules were subjected to the same rigorous testing as the failed SACseat. Here, a capsule is mounted on the front of a rocket-powered sled prior to a high-speed ground test. Note the large window on the clamshell door. *American Aviation Historical Society*

A different escape capsule from the one in the preceding photo, marked "Stanley IX," is on a rocket-equipped test sled. This capsule lacks the window on the clamshell door. On the real escape capsules, once the crewman initiated an ejection, mechanisms in the capsule raised the crewman's legs and drew in his feet, tightened the restraint harness, and snapped the clamshell door shut. *American Aviation Historical Society*

A Stanley escape capsule has just been launched from the center cabin of a YB/RB-58A during static testing at Edwards Air Force Base, California. Two rockets on the rear of the capsule lifted it from the aircraft. Once the capsule cleared the aircraft, parachutes automatically were deployed. *American Aviation Historical Society*

Warrant Officer Edward J. Murray, in the light-colored suit to the right, has just emerged from a Stanley escape capsule following the first air-launched test of the capsule with a human subject, at Edwards Air Force Base, California, on February 28, 1962. The B-58 was flying at 565 mph at an altitude of 20,000 feet when the capsule was ejected.

The Stanley escape capsule was designed to float should it happen to land on water, allowing the occupant to survive until he could egress or be rescued. A controlled flotation test is being conducted on a capsule, showing the clamshell doors. *San Diego Air and Space Museum*

A crewman is emerging from a Stanley escape capsule after a water-landing test. When the capsule touched down on water, flotation cells were activated, preventing the capsule from sinking. *San Diego Air and Space Museum*

A Convair YB/RB-58A is landing at Edwards Air Force Base, California, on March 7, 1958. The tail number is faint, but it appears to be 5665, which would equate to serial number 55-665.

Serial number 55-662 is seen after being converted from the NB-58A to a TB-58A trainer. This was one of several YB/RB-58As that were converted to TB-58As. Among other tasks, this plane served as a chase plane for test flights of the XB-70A at Edwards Air Force Base. *American Aviation Historical Society*

Fitzhugh L. "Fitz" Fulton, *second from left*, his flight crew, and an unidentified officer to the left are conferring alongside Convair YB/RB-58A, serial number 55-662. Fitz Fulton (1925–2015) was a test pilot at Edwards Air Force Base and was a project pilot for the B-58. He and his crew set an international altitude record of 85,360 feet in a B-58 in 1962, with the Hustler carrying a payload of 11,023 pounds. *Defense Visual Information Center*

With an MB-1 parked on a trolley to the side, the tall and somewhat gangly landing gear of YB/RB-58A, serial number 55-662, is accentuated. Despite its awkward appearance, the landing gear of the Hustlers was generally considered sufficiently robust and dependable. However, the tires were prone to anomalies and blowouts until metal wheels called rolling flanges were introduced. These were interspersed with the stock wheels and ensured that the plane would continue to roll in the event of tire failures. *American Aviation Historical Society*

By the time this close-up view of the side of the cockpit of the third Hustler, serial number 55-662, was taken, the plane's designation on the data stencil had been amended from YB/RB-58A to NB-58A. This change was effected when the plane was used for flight-testing the General Electric YJ93 turbojet engine, in support of the XB-70 Valkyrie program. Also below the windscreen is the insignia of the Air Research and Development Command (ARDC). *American Aviation Historical Society*

Convair NB-58A, serial number 55-662, originally YB/RB-58A, is depicted during testing of the General Electric YJ93 turbojet engine, which is mounted under the belly of the aircraft. This single-shaft axial-flow turbojet engine featured a variable-stator compressor and a fully variable convergent/divergent exhaust nozzle. *American Aviation Historical Society*

In a left-side view of NB-58A, serial number 55-662, the front of the YJ93 engine is visible under the fuselage. The vertical tail had been repainted in red, with a black (or possibly dark blue) arrow edged in white and the insignia of the Air Force Flight Test Center superimposed. The wingtips were red, edged in white. *American Aviation Historical Society*

The J93 nacelle is viewed from the front right, also providing a clear view of how the covers for the J79 nacelles fit over the tips of the inlet spikes. The J93 engine weighed about 6,000 pounds and had a maximum thrust of 31,500 pounds at sea level. *American Aviation Historical Society*

From the side, the front of the J93 nacelle had a pronounced shark's-mouth profile. In addition to the red intake covers on the J79 nacelles' intakes, a small protective cap was fastened to the tip of the inlet spike, the conical element inside the intake. *American Aviation Historical Society*

Convair NB-58A, serial number 55-662, is viewed from the front, with the big YJ93 engine slung under the fuselage. This engine produced a maximum sea-level thrust of 28,800 pounds-force (lbs.-f), compared to this aircraft's General Electric YJ79-GE-5B engines, each of which delivered a maximum of 15,600 lbs.-f at sea level. *American Aviation Historical Society*

The empennage of NB-58A, serial number 55-662, is viewed from the right rear, including details of the tail cone and the dummy radome on the lower part of the vertical tail. A red plug to keep out foreign objects is installed on the left outboard engine exhaust nozzle. *American Aviation Historical Society*

Among other achievements during its test flight career, Convair YB/RB-58A, serial number 55-663, construction number 4, was the first Hustler to drop a weapons pod at Mach 1, on September 20, 1957, and the first to drop a pod at Mach 2, on December 20, 1957. Under the outboard right engine nacelle is a camera pod. *Stan Piet collection*

In a photo of the pilot's cockpit of an early Hustler with the SACseat, not the crew capsule, note how the seat, rudder pedals, and control stick are offset slightly to the left of the center. This was to provide better visibility around the center column of the windscreen. On the console to the left is the throttle quadrant. The rudder pedals are embossed with the word "Convair" and a simple representation of a B-58.
*National Museum of the United States Air Force*

The main instrument panel (*center*) and the fuel control panel (*right*) of an early B-58 cockpit are shown. "B-58" is written in raised figures on the bottom of each rudder pedal. The left side of the main instrument panel included flight instruments and gauges as well as such items as a UHF channel indicator and ram-air temperature gauge. The right side of the main panel contained four vertical columns of controls and gauges for the four engines, at the tops of which were engine-fire detector circuit-test buttons. Below these buttons were gauges for various engine and fuel systems. To the right, part of the fuel control panel is visible.

More of the fuel control panel is visible in this view of an early B-58 with a SACseat. The Hustler had a complex fuel system, and the pilot was tasked with its management via this panel. It was important to keep fuel distributed properly in the various fuel tanks in the wings, fuselage, and weapons pod, to maintain the aircraft's center of gravity.

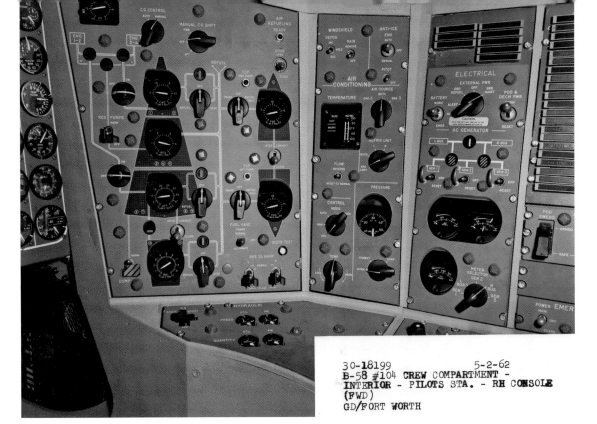

On the right side of the pilot's cockpit are, *left to right*, the fuel control panel, air conditioning and deicing control panel, and electrical control panel. Controls for the hydraulic system are on the console at the bottom. This photo and the three that follow were taken in B-58A, serial number 61-2068 (airframe no. 104), on May 2, 1962. *National Museum of the United States Air Force*

30-18199                    5-2-62
B-58 #104 CREW COMPARTMENT -
INTERIOR - PILOTS STA. - RH CONSOLE
(FWD)
GD/FORT WORTH

The right side of the cockpit is depicted with the seat removed. To the upper right is a compartment for storing ejection seat safety pins, below which is stored a folded-up sun shield. The niche below the sun shield is for storing food packs. *National Museum of the United States Air Force*

30-18194                    5-2-62
B-58 #104 CREW COMPARTMENT -
INTERIOR - PILOTS STA. - RH SIDE
GD/FORT WORTH

The pilot's cockpit of B-58A, serial number 61-2068, is viewed through the hatch with the SACseat removed, showing the side consoles, the control stick, part of the main instrument panel, and, at the bottom, the ejection rails for the pilot's SACseat. *National Museum of the United States Air Force*

30-18195                    5-2-62
B-58 #104 CREW COMPARTMENT -
INTERIOR - PILOTS STA. - PLAN VIEW
GD/FORT WORTH

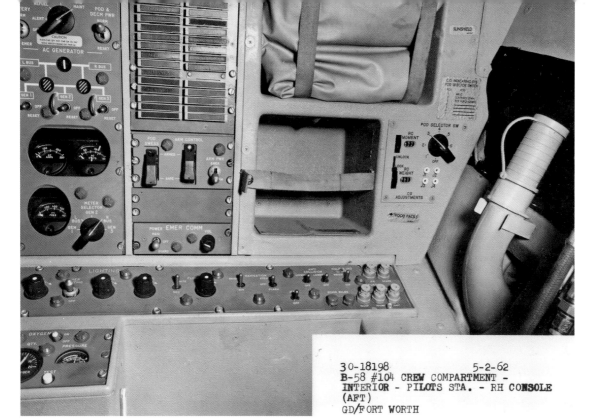

The rear of the right side of the pilot's cockpit is shown close-up, including part of the electrical panel, the stored sunscreen, the storage niche for food packs, and center-of-gravity control panel. To the left of the sunscreen is the warning and caution lamp panel. On the console toward the bottom are lighting switches. *National Museum of the United States Air Force*

30-18198                    5-2-62
B-58 #104 CREW COMPARTMENT -
INTERIOR - PILOTS STA. - RH CONSOLE
(AFT)
GD/FORT WORTH

On the left side of a B-58 pilot's cockpit, along the upper side is the autopilot control panel, below which are the pilot's left sidewall console (which includes engine-starting controls) and lower left console. *National Museum of the United States Air Force*

The left side of the cockpit of B-58A, serial number 61-2068, is viewed with the pilot's seat removed. Next to the rear of the side window is a loop at the end of an escape rope, for emergency escapes on the ground. To the upper left are a compartment and door for storing the aircraft's flight records and the rewind mechanism for the escape rope. *National Museum of the United States Air Force*

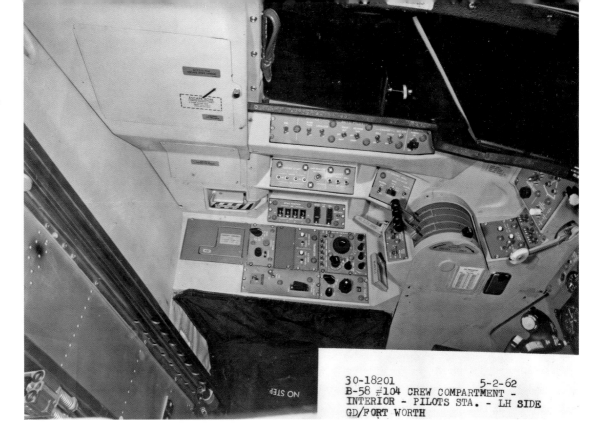

30-18201                5-2-62
B-58 #104 CREW COMPARTMENT -
INTERIOR - PILOTS STA. - LH SIDE
GD/FORT WORTH

In another photo of the left side of a B-58 pilot's cockpit, taken on June 6, 1960, the SAC seat is installed and is visible at the bottom of the photo. *National Museum of the United States Air Force*

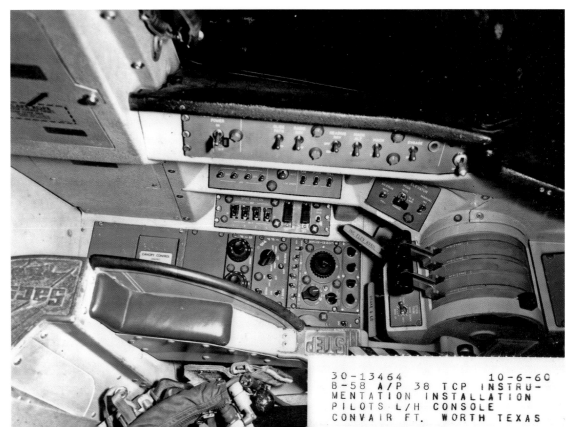

30-13464                10-6-60
B-58 A/P 38 TCP INSTRU-
MENTATION INSTALLATION
PILOTS L/H CONSOLE
CONVAIR FT. WORTH TEXAS

The bombardier/navigator was seated in the center cabin of the B-58. This photo shows the forward right corner of that compartment in B-58A, serial number 61-2068, on May 2, 1962. To the left is the navigation control panel, which forms the lower right corner of the larger navigator's main instrument panel. The small, trapezoidal panel at the upper center is the navigator's auxiliary flight instrument panel, to the right of which is the loop grip at the end of the escape rope. At the lower center is the control stick of the tracking and flight-controller unit. *National Museum of the United States Air Force*

This is the bombardier/navigator's main instrument panel in B-58A, serial number 61-2068. The main panel is divided into nine individual panels, on three tiers. On the top tier are, *left to right*, the indicator panel, the offset and storage panel, and the malfunction control panel. On the center tier are the astro control panel, the search radar indicator panel and scope, and the upper part of the navigation control panel. On the lower tier are the weapon monitor and release panel, the ballistics control panel, and the lower part of the navigation control panel. *National Museum of the United States Air Force*

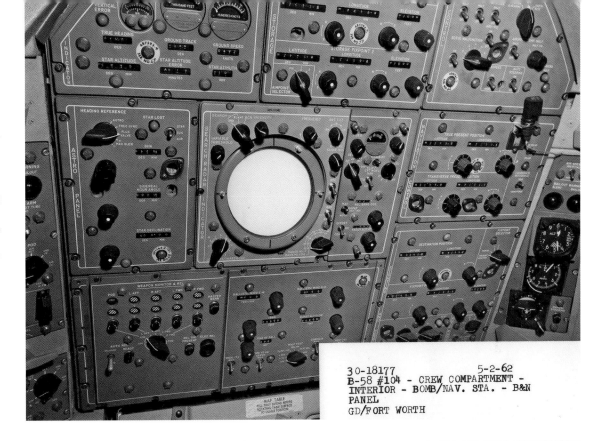

The defense systems operator (DSO), who operated the Hustler's active and passive defense systems, sat in the aft cabin of the B-58. This May 1962 photo in B-58A, serial number 61-2068, shows a small portion of the left side of the DSO's compartment. At the top is the left side panel, below which is the canopy jettison handle. At the bottom is the left console; toward the forward end of the console is the ball-shaped manual-control handle for the tail turret, situated on the manual-control panel. *National Museum of the United States Air Force*

Convair YB/RB-58A airframe 4A (as opposed to airframe 4) was never completed but was selected to serve as a static-test article, to be subjected to gradually increasing stresses in a laboratory setting until destruction. To transport the airframe from Carswell Air Force Base, Texas, to the test site at Wright-Patterson Air Force Base in Ohio, a B-36F was modified to carry the airframe under its belly. The combination of B-36F and airframe 4A is seen on that flight on March 12, 1957. *National Archives*

Airframe 4A is slung under the B-36F during the final approach to Wright-Patterson Air Force Base on March 12, 1957. It was necessary to remove the mother ship's two inboard propellers for this mission. *American Aviation Historical Society*

As seen from the rear of the left wing of the B-36F mother ship, airframe 4A is attached to special shackles in the bomb bay, and antisway braces are attached to the wing roots of the airframe. The tail of the fuselage and the vertical tail were not installed for the flight from Carswell to Wright-Patterson. *National Museum of the United States Air Force*

Airframe A4 is positioned in a test rack in a hangar at Wright-Patterson Air Force Base. Here, the airframe was subjected to gradually increasing structural forces until it was destroyed, as part of a study of the stresses the airframe could endure during flight. The wings with the engine nacelles and the vertical tail had been reinstalled. *National Museum of the United States Air Force*

By February 9, 1962, when this overhead photo of airframe 4A was taken during stress tests at Wright-Patterson Air Force Base, the right wing had finally failed, separating completely from the fuselage. The failure occurred at 135 percent of the wing's design ultimate load: 100 percent design ultimate load is the structure's failure limit, as designed. Note the open hatch of the DSO's compartment atop the forward fuselage. *National Museum of the United States Air Force*

During the static tests at Wright-Patterson Air Force Base, B-58 airframe 4A was stress-tested to destruction. The airframe was photographed from below and to the rear on March 26, 1962, after the point of destruction had been reached. *National Museum of the United States Air Force*

The fifth Hustler to be produced, YB/RB-58A USAF, serial number 55-0664, is undergoing in-flight refueling from a Boeing KC-135. This Hustler first flew on November 30, 1957, and was used in load testing and in-flight-refueling tests. *American Aviation Historical Society*

Convair YB/RB-58A, serial number 55-666, first flew on March 20, 1958, and was used in a number of test programs, including that for the YJ79-GE-5 engine. For years this Hustler was on static display at Chanute Air Force Base, Illinois. In 2017, it was transferred to the Castle Air Museum, Atwater, California, and is reportedly being restored. In this photo, there are two sealed-beam landing lights, one on the drag link on each side of the nose landing-gear strut. Above the left-hand landing light is sealed-beam taxi light.
*American Aviation Historical Society*

YB/RB-58A, serial number 55-666, was photographed from the left side, probably on the same occasion as the preceding photo, judging from some of the small details common between the two photos. The actuating cylinders for the pilot's and DSO's hatch doors are in view. *American Aviation Historical Society*

In a photo ostensibly of YB/RB-58A, serial number 55-666, on the same occasion as the two preceding photos, details of the right main landing gear are in view. At the bottom of the gear was a bogie unit with two axles, each of which held two dual wheels. Above the wheels was a substantial shock strut, attached at the top by means of a pivoting mechanism to a W-truss column assembly. This construction permitted the shock strut and wheels to pivot so as to clear the weapons pod when being retracted or lowered. The diagonal structure to the front of the shock strut was the drag strut. *American Aviation Historical Society*

Originally YB/RB-58A, serial number 55-670, this plane was the first to be converted to a TB-58A trainer, and it is that version that is seen here taking off from an airbase, bearing the insignia of the 43rd Bombardment Wing and the blue sash with white stars of Strategic Air Command on the forward fuselage. The TB-58A replaced the small windows in the middle cabin with two new windows on each side and two on top of the compartment for better visibility for the instructor pilot, who sat in that compartment. The pilot trainee sat in the front cockpit, and an observer, usually a pilot working on his proficiency, was in the aft cabin. *Stan Piet collection*

TB-58 TAKE-OFF WITH POD SHOWING WINDOW CONFIGURATION

The first Hustler converted to a TB-58A, serial number 55-670, lifts off from a runway. It was necessary to field a trainer version of the Hustler because of the bomber's character as a high-performance aircraft and its unique handling properties. In all, eight TB-58As were converted. *National Museum of the United States Air Force*

The Convair TB-58A was a basic YB-58 modified for the pilot-training role, including the conversion of the middle crew cabin to the instructor pilot's cockpit. The instructor pilot had a nonencapsulated ejection seat and full flight controls. The seat was offset to the right of the center of the compartment to allow him improved forward vision. The compartment had more side and overhead windows than in the B-58.

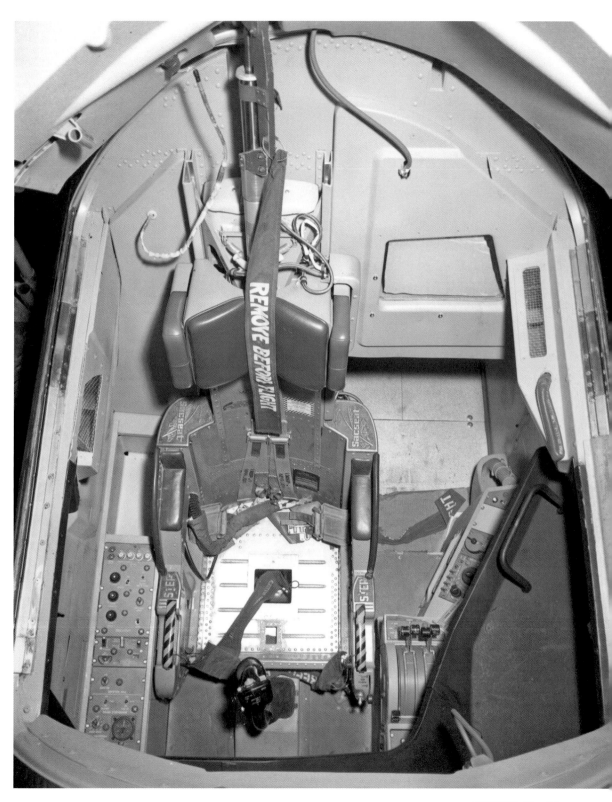

The center cabin or cockpit, also called the second station, of the TB-58A was assigned to the instructor pilot. Whereas the pilot trainee's seat in the forward cockpit, or first station, was offset to the left of center, the instructor pilot's seat was offset to the right, so that he could see past the pilot trainee through the opening above the upper right of his instrument panel, permitting a forward view through the windscreen. *San Diego Air and Space Museum*

The aft cabin, or third station, was reserved for an observer, who typically was a B-58 pilot working on his proficiency. This is the observer's view through a window in bulkhead 3.5, with the instructor pilot's instrument panel and control stick visible through it. In the left background may be seen a man in a light-colored civilian shirt seated in the forward cockpit. *San Diego Air and Space Museum*

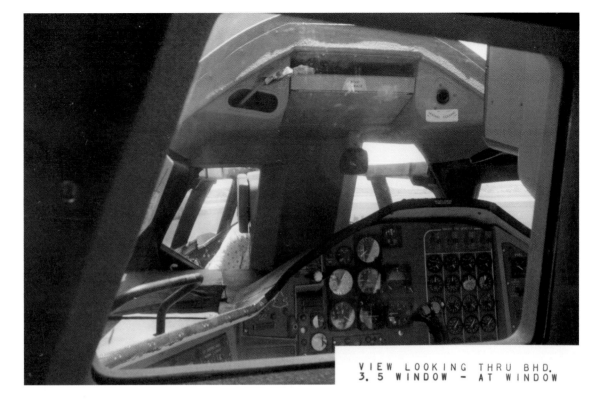

VIEW LOOKING THRU BHD.
3. 5 WINDOW – AT WINDOW

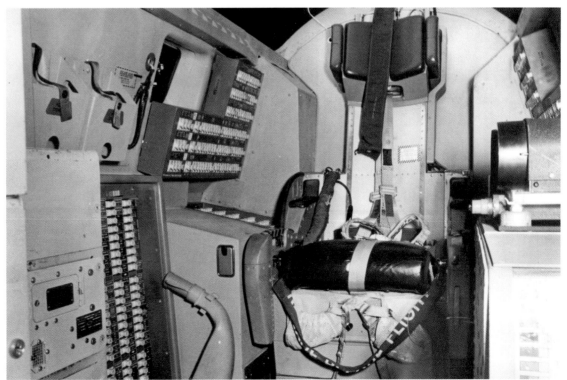

In the third station, the SACseat is viewed from the front, with the right and left AC power panels to the sides. This seat was located on the fore-and-aft centerline. There was a crawlspace between the second and third stations so that the occupants could trade places if necessary. *San Diego Air and Space Museum*

VIEW LOOKING FWD FROM
OBSERVER - 3RD STA. -
NORMAL HEAD POSITION

In a view from the observer's seat in the third station, there was only one forward window, on the left side, below which was the crawlspace to the second station. At the top is the bailout alert and warning panel. *San Diego Air and Space Museum*

Convair YB/RB-58A, serial number 55-672, is seen from a chase plane during a flight after the plane became the second to be converted to a TB-58A. During its time as a trainer, the plane was assigned at least two successive nicknames: "Lucky 13" and "Sweet Sadness."

A flight-line crewman is directing a TB-58A into a parking position during summer training exercises of US Air Force Academy cadets at Little Rock Air Force Base, Arkansas, during July 1968. The bulges on the bottoms of the engine nacelles were designed to fit around gearboxes on the bottoms of the J79 engines.

# CHAPTER 2

# B-58A

The first production B-58, serial number 58-1023, made its first flight in September 1959. The full-production aircraft differed from the YB-58s in details. The structure of the first seventeen YB-58 aircraft was different from the production aircraft, and the landing gear of all thirty differed as well.

As B-58 production ramped up, but due to funding not being to the level that was desired, the fate of the YB-58 aircraft was considered. Ultimately, the decision was made to bring the late YB-58 aircraft up to operational standard. This modification program was known as "Junior Flash-Up."

Another modification program was instituted for the earlier aircraft, which could not reasonably be brought up to operational-aircraft standard. Instead, these were converted to TB-58 configuration. The second seat of the TB-58 became the instructor pilot's seat and was offset slightly to provide a modest amount of forward vision.

On October 26, the last of the 116 Hustlers built, serial number 61-2080, was delivered to the 305th Bomb Wing.

The first operational B-58 unit, the 43rd Bomb Wing (SAC), was activated at Davis-Monthan Air Force Base and was immediately transferred to Carswell Air Force Base, adjoining the Convair plant, on March 1, 1960. In September 1964, the 43rd and its Hustlers moved from Texas to Little Rock Air Force Base, Arkansas. The unit remained there throughout the rest of the Hustlers' service life.

In September 1960, a second wing was activated. Based at Bunker Hill Air Force Base, Indiana, the 305th Bomb Wing would operate the B-58 until January 16, 1970.

During the Hustler's decade of service, men flying the bomber set nineteen world speed records, including the longest supersonic flight in history—Tokyo to London—taking 8 hours, 35 minutes, 20.4 seconds to cover 8,028 miles. That record, set October 16, 1963, still stands.

While the B-58 never delivered a payload to enemy soil, it was an effective deterrent. One mechanism used to reinforce US air supremacy to the public—and the enemy—was record-setting flights. Among these:

**January 12, 1961**. Maj. E. J. Deutschendorf, Capt. William Polthemus, and Capt. Raymond Wagener flew B-58, serial number 59-0442, carrying a 4,409-pound (2,000 kg) payload over the AFFTC's 1,240-mile (2,000 km) course, setting a world speed record of 1,061.808 mph. The flight also broke the existing world speed records for the same distance with a 2,205-pound (1,000 kg) payload and with no payload. Maj. Deutschendorf's son incidentally would also become famous, using the stage name John Denver.

**January 14, 1961**. B-58, serial number 59-2441, flown by Lt. Col. Harold Confer with Lt. Col. Richard Weir and Maj. Howard Bialas, set three international speed-with-payload records by flying at a speed of 1284.73 mph over a 621-mile (1,000 km) closed circuit, winning the 1961 Thompson Trophy.

**May 10, 1961**. B-58, serial number 59-2451, flown by Maj. Elmer E. Murphy, Maj. Eugene Moses, and defense systems operator (DSO), Lt. David Dickerson, won Aero Club of France's Bleriot Cup, flying 669.4 miles (1,078 km) in 30 minutes and 45 seconds, at an average speed of 1,302 mph. Sadly, this crew was killed two weeks later in a crash.

**1961**. Mackay Trophy awarded to Lt. Col. William Payne, Maj. William Polthemus, and Maj. Raymond Wagener, in B-58, serial number 59-2451, for their historic nonstop flight from Carswell AFB, Texas, to Paris, France, which culminated in the establishment of two international speed records.

**1962**. Mackay Trophy awarded to Maj. Robert Sowers and Capts. Robert MacDonald and John Walton for most meritorious flight of the year, on March 5, 1961, flying serial number 59-2458 round trip between New York and Los Angeles in 4 hours, 42 minutes.

**1962**. Bendix Trophy awarded to Maj. Robert Sowers and Capts. Robert MacDonald and John Walton, who flew from Los Angeles to New York City in the Convair B-58A Hustler, serial number 59-2458, in 2 hours and 56.8 seconds, an average speed of 1,214.17 mph. This record would stand for twenty-eight years.

**1962**. Harmon Trophy awarded to Maj. Fitzhugh Fulton, Capt. William R. Payne, and civilian flight test engineer C. R. Haines, who took B-58A, serial number 59-2456, to 85,360.84 feet with an 11,023-pound (5,000 kg) load on September 18, 1962.

In late 1965, citing costs, Secretary of Defense Robert McNamara ordered retirement of the B-58 by 1970. Although the Air Force objected, the requirement was met in January 1970. Other than those examples preserved in museums, the aircraft that had been consigned to storage at Davis-Monthan were reduced to scrap in 1977.

Flight crewmen in bright-orange flight suits and white helmets stand to the front of B-58A-10-CF, serial number 59-2456. Behind the crewmen are a tail turret assembly with an M61 20 mm rotary cannon, mounted on a trolley and with 20 mm ammo belts arranged on the ground adjacent to the turret, and four Mk. 43 variable-yield thermonuclear bombs. Also present is a two-component pod (TCP), which is shown disassembled. The lower component, to the left and numbered B-2-4, has an indentation on top for fitting against the upper component, which is numbered B-3-6 and has colorful paintwork and black stripes for easier tracking during drop tests. *Stan Piet collection*

Convair Hustlers are undergoing construction on the assembly line in Plant 4, Fort Worth, Texas. In the closest two airframes, the forward fuselage and aft fuselage and vertical tail have been installed; on the closer airframe, scaffolding is around the tail.

Hustler airframes are on the final-assembly line at Plant 4. Engine nacelles were installed before final assembly, on the major-mating line, but the engines were installed in the nacelles during final assembly. A tail number is present on the nearest plane but is indistinct: it may have been 92428, which equated to B-58A serial number 59-2428.

The nose and main landing gears have been installed on this Hustler. Frisket paper is still on the forward fuselage. Framing for the windscreen is in place, but the glass panels have not been installed. The large, rectangular openings on the wings are where the upper fairings of the main landing-gear wells will be installed.

Rolling scaffolding surrounds B-58As on the final-assembly line at Plant 4. The second airframe is serial number 59-2430, which signified this was a B-58A-10-CF, the suffix "10" referring to production block 10, and "CF" standing for the manufacturer, Convair–Fort Worth. This plane was accepted by the US Air Force on January 28, 1960. Crew compartment hatch doors have not been installed on the two closest airframes, but the aft one is present on the third one.

Convair B-58A-10-CF, serial number 59-2439, is at the front of the line of nearly completed Hustlers at Plant 4. The plane's construction number, "42," is painted on the forward fuselage and the upper part of the vertical tail, and the tail number, 92439, also is present. Note how the nosewheels are on a small lift platform. *American Aviation Historical Society*

Partway through B-58 production, underwing pylons were introduced, permitting the aircraft to carry four Mk. 43 variable-yield thermonuclear bombs in addition to carrying the weapons pod. Two of the bombs are present on pylons under the right wing, and the rear of a bomb under the left wing is visible in the background. *American Aviation Historical Society*

Technicians are making connections on a single-component weapons pod under the belly of a B-58 Hustler. A standard accessory was a trailer for transporting the weapons pod on the ground. The pod rested on cradles, which were raised hydraulically for coupling the pod to the aircraft. Note the covers over the main landing gear to the sides of the photo. *National Museum of the United States Air Force*

A two-component pod is installed under a B-58. The lower component was a fuel pod, designated BLU 2/B-2. On the upper rear of the lower component is the kicker: a vertical fin that contacted the fuselage, to provide a fulcrum for the safe dropping of the lower component so as not to damage the upper component. The two upper fins of the upper component are to the front of the kicker; not visible here is the lower, retractable fin. *American Aviation Historical Society*

The three-man flight crew of a B-58 is running from a station wagon to their aircraft during a scramble. This photo includes a clear view of the tail stinger, featuring an M61 (originally T171E3) 20 mm Vulcan cannon, a rotary six-barrel design with a rate of fire of up to 4,000 rounds per minute. Above the gun is the radome for the Emerson fire-control radar, which aimed the gun. *National Museum of the United States Air Force*

An MB-1 single-component, free-fall weapons pod is slung under YB/RB-58A-10-CF, serial number 58-1011. In the foreground, a two-component pod is on a trailer; a crane is lowering the upper component onto the lower one. This aircraft was the first Hustler to drop a pod by using a fully functional navigation/bombardment system, on February 12, 1960. *National Museum of the United States Air Force*

Ground crewmen are preparing a single-component weapons pod on its trailer for mounting under a B-58. *National Museum of the United States Air Force*

A single-component weapons pod is being positioned under B-58A-10-CF, serial number 59-2448. In the background, to the right of the Hustler's right main landing gear, the tail of a Boeing B-52 is protruding through a hole in the doors of a hangar. On the upper part of the vertical tail, next to the top of the rudder, is a rear-warning radar antenna. *National Museum of the United States Air Force*

The nickname "Shackbuster" is painted on the forward fuselage of B-58A-10-CF, serial number 59-2436. To the front of the "Shackbuster" inscription is the plane's construction number, "38." After this plane participated in pod-drop tests, it was assigned to the 43rd Bombardment Wing. It is seen here with the upper of a TCP numbered B-1-11 mounted under the belly, and the lower component, B-2-16, is on a trailer.

In a photograph probably taken while the plane was on bailment to Convair for Phase 1 multiple-weapons-capability testing, B-58A-10-CF, serial number 59-2456, is armed with a weapons pod numbered B-2-15 and four pylon-mounted bombs. *National Museum of the United States Air Force*

A B-58 carrying a weapons pod is viewed from below during flight. Note the various shades of the skin panels of the aircraft. The exhaust nozzles of the engines were of variable-area design and are seen here in a constricted position. *American Aviation Historical Society*

Convair B-58A-10-CF, serial number 59-2455, was assigned to the 43rd Bombardment Wing at Carswell Air Force Base. On the opposite side of the plane, three flight crewmen are running from a civilian-type station wagon during a scramble: a procedure in which the crew gets the plane into the air as quickly as possible. *American Aviation Historical Society*

A photo of a scramble includes an excellent view of a boarding ladder, with a boom and hoist on top and sufficient room on the platform to enable easy access to all three crew hatches. This plane was B-58A-10-CF, serial number 59-2442; its nickname, "Untouchable," and the sash and shield of Strategic Air Command are on the side of the forward fuselage. *National Museum of the United States Air Force*

The crew of B-58A-15-CF, serial number 59-2455, is scrambling. Under the fuselage is weapons pod number B-1108. The round shape on the top of the fuselage between the cockpit and the bombardier/navigator's cabin is the AN/ARC-57 UHF command-radio antenna. Note the white reference markings to the front of the in-air refueling receptacle, to the front of the windscreen; these helped the flying-boom operator in the tanker line up the boom with the receptacle. *National Museum of the United States Air Force*

Three members of a flight crew just arrived in a 1959 Ford Country Sedan station wagon marked "ALERT FORCE" on the front of the hood are scrambling to their B-58. In the event of the sudden outbreak of a nuclear war, it would be imperative to get crews and strategic bombers in the air as quickly as possible, lest they be destroyed on the ground during a first strike; scrambles were rehearsed incessantly during the Cold War. *National Museum of the United States Air Force*

On the basis of the identical oil stains on the hardstand in this photo and in the preceding photos of the scrambling crew of B-58A-15-CF, serial number 59-2455, the plane in this photo is almost certainly the same one. For scrambles, the Strategic Air Command developed its minimum-interval takeoff (MITO) techniques on the basis of launching bombers such as B-58s at intervals of as little as twelve seconds. *National Museum of the United States Air Force*

A final photo of a MITO scramble drill taken above the left wing of a Hustler shows two of the crewmen running for the access ladder on the opposite side of the aircraft. The alert vehicles typically were painted blue, with a flashing red light on top of them; one alert vehicle would be assigned to each flight crew during their alert periods. *National Museum of the United States Air Force*

A B-58 Hustler with a weapons pod installed is parked under an open-ended shelter of a type nicknamed Hustler hut, at an unidentified air base. A sign on the front of the shelter warns that an explosives-loaded aircraft is inside. The sign in the foreground identifies this as a "no lone zone" and a category 2 restricted area, which meant that two men had to be in control of the aircraft, to lessen the chance that a single rogue crewman could initiate an unauthorized launch. *National Museum of the United States Air Force*

In a nighttime photograph, seven B-58s (including one for which only the left wing is visible to the left) are parked in open-ended shelters at an airbase. The Hustler huts had open fronts and backs and were fabricated from corrugated metal over metal frames; unlike hardened shelters for aircraft, they were for keeping out the elements only. *National Museum of the United States Air Force*

In another view taken at night, a B-58 is undergoing maintenance, which went on around the clock. The location was Carswell Air Force Base, Texas. The photo is undated but was released for publication in April 1964. *National Museum of the United States Air Force*

Airman Arturo Calvillo of the 43rd Bombardment Wing is servicing a B-58's defense system during a late-night maintenance session at Carswell Air Force Base. Below the radome in the foreground is the tail cone that contains the 20 mm Vulcan cannon. To allow the cannon to fire 30 degrees from the center in elevation and azimuth, the cone was of articulating design, with concentric aluminum rings that were spring-loaded against each other. *National Museum of the United States Air Force*

Airmen Atchley Cox, *left*, and James Fails of the 43rd Bombardment Wing at Carswell Air Force Base are preparing a General Electric J79 turbojet engine for installation in a B-58 in or around 1964. It usually took a couple of hours to install an engine in a Hustler. *National Museum of the United States Air Force*

General Electric displayed this J79 at a public exhibition, the spectators providing a sense of the size of the engine. The seventeen-stage compressor that is central to the design of this single-spool turbojet is clearly visible. The J79 would remain in production for more than thirty years and would provide the power for not only the B-58, but also the F-4 Phantom II, F-104 Starfighter, and A-5 Vigilante.

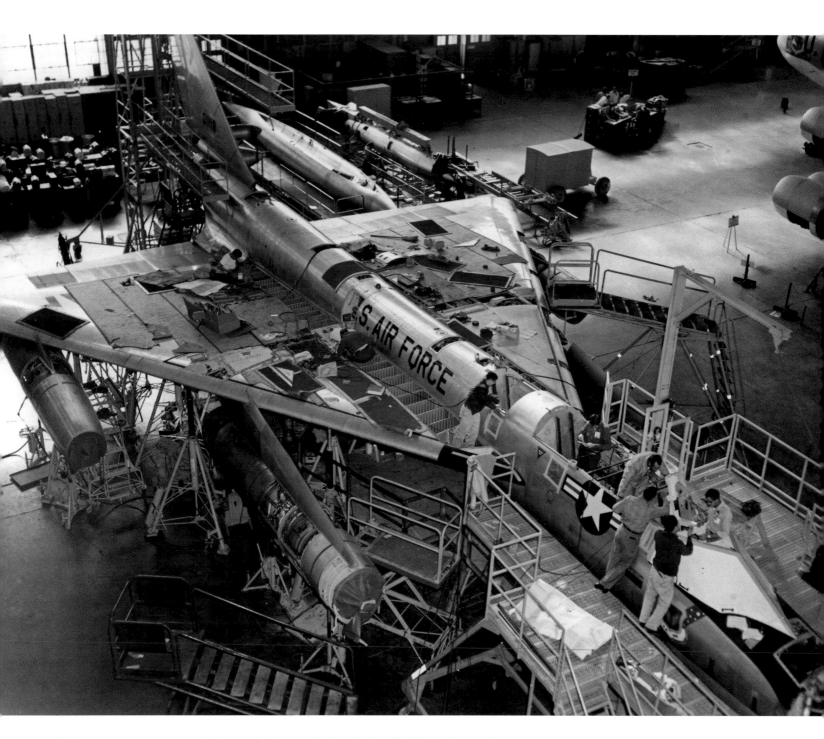

A B-58 is undergoing a major overhaul by the San Antonio Air Material Area (SAAMA) at Kelly Air Force Base, the sole depot-level overhaul shop for B-58s. Numerous skin panels have been removed from the wings and fuselage, and the crew cabins are receiving extensive work. Note the lower component of a two-component weapons pod to the rear of the left wing. *National Museum of the United States Air Force*

A deceleration parachute system was installed in the B-58 to retard landing speed. The drag chute is deployed in this view of B-58A-10-CF, serial number 59-2436, which is maintaining a nose-high attitude to further reduce the aircraft's speed by using drag. This Hustler was the first one accepted by the Air Force to have complete tactical systems installed. The plane served with the 43rd Bombardment Wing. *American Aviation Historical Society*

Convair B-58A-10-CF, serial number 59-2429, has rolled to a stop, drag chute billowing behind it. The 28-foot-diameter drag chute was housed in a compartment in the tail, fitted with two clamshell doors. *American Aviation Historical Society*

A two-component pod is installed under a B-58A, and bombs are mounted on the pylons under the wings. The top component of the TCP is numbered B-3-1. The aircraft's tail number is faint but appears to be 92456. *Stan Piet collection*

Convair B-58A-10-CF, serial number 59-2434, bore the nickname "Cannonball" during its operational career. It was the first Hustler to enter the Flash-Up program: a series of modifications and improvements to existing airframes. Visible on the forward fuselage is the SAC sash (blue with white stars) and the insignia of the 43rd Bombardment Wing. *American Aviation Historical Society*

The hatch doors of all three crew cabins of a B-58 Hustler are open and the crewmen are in their seats in this overhead view. The cabins are equipped with SACseats. The large, circular shape between the first two cabins is the AN/ARC-57 UHF command-radio antenna. *National Museum of the United States Air Force*

The pilot, navigator/bombardier, and DSO of B-58A-10-CF, serial number 58-1009, pose for their photo in their cabins. This aircraft was equipped with the Stanley escape capsules, the upper parts of which are visible. Below the exterior canopy-jettison control is painted the nickname "El Toro De Moron" along with faded artwork of a charging bull. *American Aviation Historical Society*

In an elevated view of a B-58A procured in fiscal year 1961, Stanley crew escape capsules are installed in the cabins. Over the engine intakes are FOD (foreign-object damage) screens stenciled "B-58" in light-colored paint on the fronts.

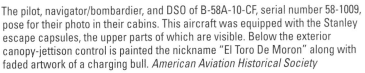

A man in civilian clothing is operating a hose with a pressure gauge coupled to one of the three gravity-feed fuel fillers atop the fuselage of a B-58. To the right is the DSO's cabin, with the upper part of the SACseat and the left AC power panel visible.

Crewmen of B-58A-20-CF, serial number 61-2060, pose for their photograph on the platform of a boarding ladder next to the crew cabins. Stanley escape capsules are present. While the crewman to the left is unidentified, the other two are G. C. Tate and Fred Voorhies.

Carrying a two-component pod under its belly, Convair B-58A-15-CF, serial number 60-1124, is poised nose-up just above a runway. This Hustler served with the 305th Bombardment Wing at Bunker Hill (later, Grissom) Air Force Base, Indiana. *National Archives*

A member of the USAF Air Police and a German shepherd are keeping watch over a line of B-58 Hustlers from the 43rd Bombardment Wing at Carswell Air Force Base, Texas, on February 9, 1961. In the foreground is B-58A-10-CF, serial number 59-2430.

Spectators get a rare glimpse of a Convair B-58 Hustler at an airshow around the late 1950s or early 1960s. Emblazoned on the side of the fuselage forward of the pilot's cockpit is the shield of the US Air Force Systems Command. *American Aviation Historical Society*

At another air show, a weapons pod on a trailer is poised underneath the fuselage of a B-58. A fabric cover to keep out foreign objects is on the exhaust outlet of the engine nacelle in the foreground. The stub pylon of the outboard nacelle is visible. *American Aviation Historical Society*

A B-58A at rest on a tarmac at a desert air base. All of the canopies are open. The pilot sits in his cockpit, but the navigator/bombardier and the defense systems operator in white helmets and orange flight suits are standing up in their cabins to beat the heat. *American Aviation Historical Society*

At one time, Convair B-58A-20-CF, serial number 61-2066, was assigned to the 43rd Bombardment Wing at Carswell Air Force Base, Texas, but in this photo the insignia and motto ("CAN DO") of the 305th Bombardment Wing, based at Bunker Hill Air Force Base, Indiana, are present on the forward fuselage. The last three digits of the serial number are marked on the nose landing-gear door in red. *National Museum of the United States Air Force*

TB-58A, serial number 55-672, is poised on a tarmac, with the upper component of a two-component pod mounted under the fuselage. This aircraft went under several nicknames, including "Clean Sweep / Q Twice," "Lucky 13," and "Sweet Sadness." *National Museum of the United States Air Force*

Convair TB-58A-10-CF, serial number 58-1007, cruises high above cloud cover. The nickname "Boomerang" is written diagonally in black forward of the SAC sash and insignia on the forward fuselage. At one point this trainer was nicknamed "Super Sue." *National Museum of the United States Air Force*

"Boomerang," TB-58A-10-CF, serial number 58-1007, banks right during the same flight documented in the preceding photo. Mounted on the fuselage is the upper component of a TCP. *National Museum of the United States Air Force*

A Strategic Air Command B-58 Hustler rests on an air base tarmac between missions. In the time-honored tradition, fire extinguishers are at the ready with which to put out any fires that might erupt around the aircraft. An orange cover is over the nose boom. *American Aviation Historical Society*

B-58A-20-CF, serial number 61-2066, is engaged in category 2 stability and control performance tests during a flight from Edwards Air Force Base, California, on April 20, 1964. After being bailed to Convair for flight tests, this Hustler was assigned to the 43rd Bombardment Wing.

B-58A-10-CF, serial number 59-2431, completed a Mach 2 test flight lasting seventy-eight minutes while assigned to the 6592nd Test Squadron. Later, this Hustler served with the 43rd Bombardment Wing. *Stan Piet collection*

At least fifty-five B-58s are visible in this view taken in or around 1971 at Davis-Monthan Air Force Base. Visible tail numbers reveal a range of serial numbers, from 58-1010 on the early side to the late-production 61-2064. *Stan Piet collection*

Convair B-58s by the dozens are stored behind a security fence at Davis-Monthan Air Force Base. For preservation, windscreens, windows, engines, and exhausts have been covered, and hatches sealed. The planes in the closest row have two-component pods under their bellies. *Stan Piet collection*

The M61Vulcan rotary cannons are still in the tail stingers of these B-58s in storage at Davis-Monthan Air Force Base on August 3, 1971. The tail numbers of the first six planes are visible: 92455, 12064, 01117, 12078, 92450, and 60662 (the third Hustler airframe). *National Museum of Naval Aviation*

A Convair Hustler, model and serial number unknown, is parked at Davis-Monthan on August 3, 1971. Light-colored covers are over the cockpit glass and the engine intakes. Although some efforts were made to seal openings where the elements could penetrate, the dry, desert climate also served to preserve the aircraft during storage. *National Museum of Naval Aviation*

Nicknamed "Cowtown Hustler," B-58A-15-CF, serial number 49-2458, set new world records during a transcontinental round trip named Operation Heat Rise on March 5, 1962. During the Los Angeles to New York leg, the plane averaged 1,214.65 mph, completing the trip in 2 hours and 58 seconds. "Cowtown Hustler" made the return trip to LA in 2 hours and 15 minutes, averaging 1,081 mph. The flight crew won the Bendix Trophy for the eastbound flight, and the Mackay Trophy for most meritorious flight of the year. *National Museum of the United States Air Force*

Award-winning "Cowtown Hustler," Convair B-58A-15-CF, serial number 59-2458, is preserved as a static display in the National Museum of the United States Air Force. The aircraft is equipped with a TCP. Resting on the floor alongside the pod is a Stanley escape capsule. *National Museum of the United States Air Force*

"Cowtown Hustler" is viewed from the right front. The object with the orange-colored top next to the TCP is a Stanley escape capsule with the clamshell door closed. A window is on the front of the door.

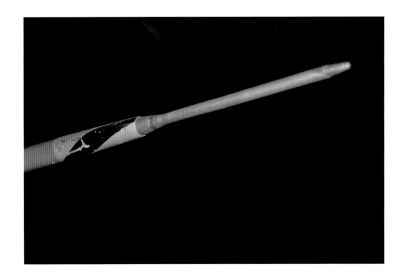

At the forward end of the nose boom, which juts from the radome on the nose of the B-58A, is the pitot tube, or pitot probe, used to determine the airspeed of the aircraft.

The B-58's landing gear, including the nose gear shown here, was hydraulically operated. It had two tubeless tires. The nose gear featured a shortened shock strut supported by two upper arms and two lower arms, all of truss-type construction. When the gear was retracted, the connections of these arms with the shock strut served as pivoting points, causing the gear to—in effect—fold, with sufficient clearance between the wheels and the nose of the weapons pod.

A sealed-beam landing light is mounted on each of the forward arms of the nose landing gear. A sealed-beam taxiing light is above the left-hand landing light.

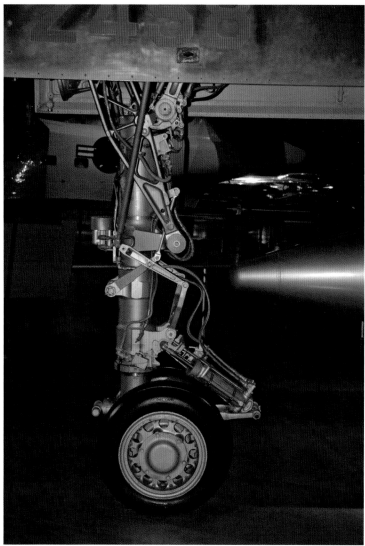

As seen in a left-side view of the nose landing gear, the forward support arms slant to the rear at their bottoms and are attached to a fitting on the center rear of the shock strut. The bottom of the left upper support arm is in view below the landing-gear-bay door and is attached to a fitting on the rear of the top of the shock strut.

The upper part of the nose gear, the three lights, and part of the gear bay are seen from the front. The doors of the nose gear were equipped with auxiliary pneumatic boost actuators, to compensate for the heavy air loads exerted on the nose-gear bay during takeoffs.

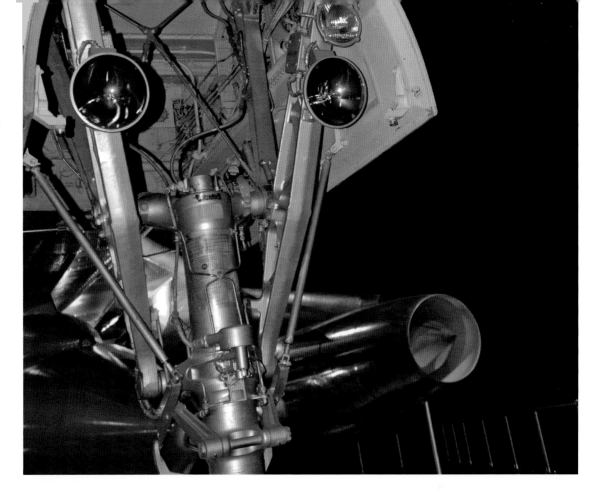

In a view of the nose landing gear of "Cowtown Hustler" from the right side, the proximity of the nose of the weapons pod to the gear and the necessity of having an articulated nose gear to get around the pod while retracting or extending are obvious.

The right nose-gear door is shown close-up, including the piano hinge that secures it to the fuselage. The two dark-colored vertical shapes above the door are AN/ALQ-16 radar track-breaker antennas: one receiver antenna and one transmitter antenna. The radar track breaker was a repeater-type jammer.

The forward part of the right wing root and the right windows for the navigator/bombardier (*right*) and the defense systems operator (*left*) of "Cowtown Hustler" are depicted. Inside the red circle is a static port, part of the pitot-static system.

On the side of the forward fuselage below the cockpit windscreen are the Strategic Air Command's sash, a blue stripe with white stars, and the insignia of the 43rd Bombardment Wing.

In a view of the underside of the right wing root, the leading edge of the wing, and the adjacent fuselage, the red object to the right is a hot-air discharge vent.

Visible in the inlet of one of "Cowtown Huster's" engines the inlet spike is clearly visible.  As installed in the Hustler, each GE J79 engine, with afterburner, could develop 15,600 pounds of thrust.

The General Electric J79 engines of the Hustlers featured an innovative variable-area exhaust nozzle, which was opened up when the engines were in afterburner.

The right inboard engine nacelle and its pylon are viewed from under the wing, with some details of the right main landing gear also evident. Near the rear of the nacelle pylon is a stencil giving the location for attaching a jack pad.

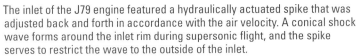

The inlet of the J79 engine featured a hydraulically actuated spike that was adjusted back and forth in accordance with the air velocity. A conical shock wave forms around the inlet rim during supersonic flight, and the spike serves to restrict the wave to the outside of the inlet.

The right main landing gear is viewed from its outboard side. Like the nose gear, the main gear featured a shortened shock strut, the top of which was attached to a column assembly. This was a complex mechanism designed to enable the gear to retract into the landing-gear bay, which had a limited height. To the right is part of the drag link.

Each main landing gear had two axles, each of which held two split-type, dual, nonfrangible wheels with a total of four tires. From 1961 onward, between the rubber tubeless tires of each dual wheel was a solid-steel wheel, called a rolling flange, designed to allow the plane to keep moving on ground if a tire blew out. All tires on the B-58 were extra-high-pressure (240 psi) Goodyear 22 × 7.7-12, rated for a minimum of ten takeoffs and landings.

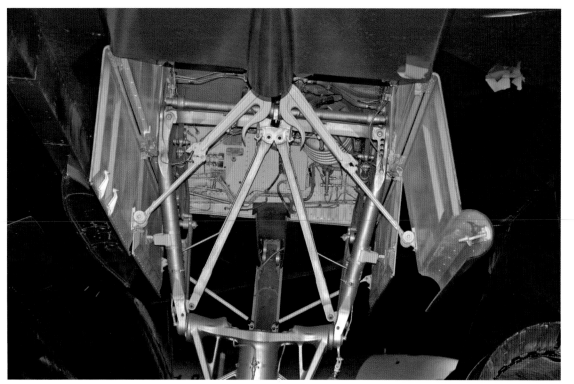

In a photo from the rear of the upper part of the right main landing gear, at the top are the bay, the bay doors, the top of the drag link, and the column assembly, also called the W truss, and at the bottom is the top of the shock strut. The landing-gear doors were mechanically opened, closed, and latched by the movement of the landing gear but were locked securely and unlocked by hydraulic power.

The column assembly, drag link (the dark object visible through the column assembly), the shock strut, and the wheels of the right landing gear are observed from the rear. Also, two rolling flanges are visible as the bright-metal objects between the dual wheels. When retracted, the shock strut pivoted on the column assembly in such way that the wheels rotated 180 degrees on their lateral axis so as to fit snugly in the landing-gear bay.

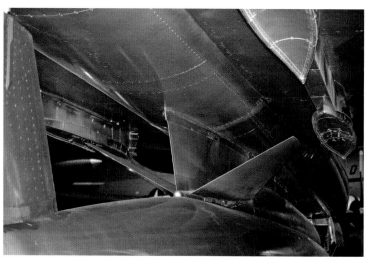

The kicker, a fin on top of the rear part of a weapons pod that contacts a fitting in the belly of the B-58, thus forming a fulcrum by which the pod can be dropped without its rear end damaging the aircraft, is depicted.

In a view along the right rear of the two-component pod mounted under "Cowtown Hustler," to the far left is the kicker, and farther forward are the two upper fins of the upper component of the TCP. To the upper right are the two right bomb pylons, while another pylon is visible in the left background.

The two-component pod mounted under "Cowtown Hustler" is viewed from the rear, with the kicker forming the vertical fin and the two top fins of the upper component of the TCP being the diagonal fins.

The upper part of the left main landing gear of "Cowtown Hustler" is seen from the rear. Note the drag links for operating the bay doors.

The upper portion of the left main landing gear is viewed from a different perspective, showing the interiors of the outboard bay doors. To the right are the two left bomb pylons, and to the left of the landing gear are the left inboard engine nozzle, nacelle, and pylon.

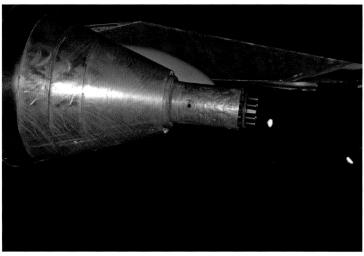

On the belly of the Hustler, between the trailing edges of the wings, are two dark-colored Plexiglas panels housing the Doppler radar transmitting and receiving units. The small, streamlined pod on the trailing edge of the wing at the upper center of the photo is an aft receiving antenna for the track-breaking jamming equipment.

The tail stinger, with the muzzles of the M61 Vulcan 20 mm rotary cannon protruding from the sleeve at the rear of the structure, is seen from the lower left side.

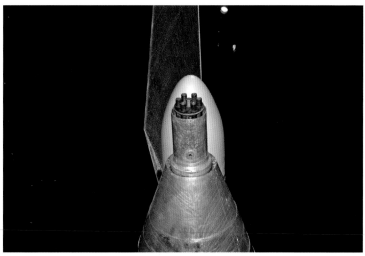

As viewed from the left rear of "Cowtown Hustler," at the top is the rudder, below which are the radome for the fire-control radar and, at the bottom, part of the tail stinger.

The 20 mm tail stinger is viewed from below with the white form of the fire-control radome above it.

In a view from below the trailing edge of the left wing of "Cowtown Hustler," the kicker of the two-component pod is prominent between the two rear bomb pylons under the fuselage. Also visible to the far right are the Plexiglas panels over the Doppler radar equipment.

The left outboard engine nacelle with the variable-area exhaust nozzle in the open position is in the foreground, with the landing gear and the TCP also in view.

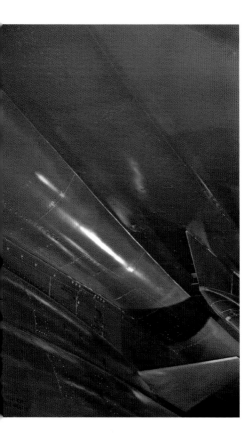

Details are shown close-up of the joint between the built-in pylon of the TCP and the bottom of the fuselage. Part of the right side of the TCP is toward the bottom of the photo, including the upper left fin of the upper component. Above the fin is the front of the left rear bob pylon.

In a photo of the forward left quarter of the two-component pod on "Cowtown Hustler," the darker area toward the bottom is the upper part of the lower component, while above it is the upper component and its built-in pylon. The junction of the two components formed a very tight seam. While the lower component was filled with fuel only, the upper component carried fuel and a warhead; the black stencil on the upper component pertains to the adjacent emergency defueling cover and depressurization plug.

The leading edge of the left wing at its junction with the fuselage is depicted, along with the left windows for the center and aft cabins. Also present are warning symbols for the ejection seats, canopy-jettisoning handles and indicator stickers, and reference marks for where to cut through the fuselage skin for emergency rescue of the navigator/bombardier.

Between the pilot's windscreen and the Strategic Air Command insignia on the left side of the forward fuselage is the data stencil of "Cowtown Hustler," listing its designation, B-58A-15-CF; the serial number, 59-2458A (the "A" suffix was an old one indicating a USAF airplane); and specifications for the fuel required for this aircraft, JP-4.

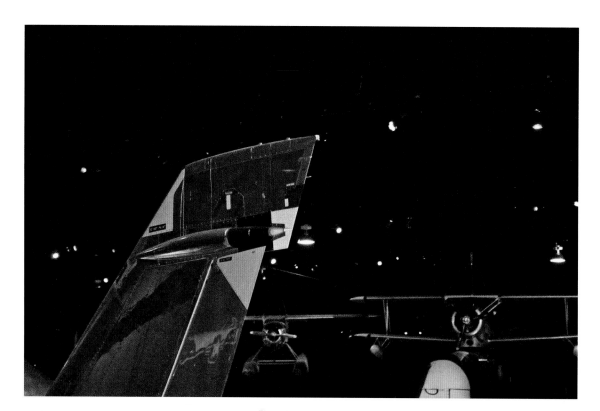

There were several inconspicuous antennas on the top of the dorsal fin of the Hustler, the most prominent one being the streamlined aft radar-warning antenna right above the top of the rudder.

In the National Museum of the United States Air Force, "Cowtown Hustler," *left*, is dwarfed by a Convair B-36J Peacemaker, the huge strategic bomber of the late 1940s and 1950s. It will be recalled that a B-36 carried under its belly the airframe of a YB/RB-58A from Carswell Air Force Base, Texas, to Wright-Patterson Air Force Base, Ohio, for static testing on May 12, 1957.

In a rear view of "Cowtown Hustler," the elevons on the wings are lowered. The control surfaces of the Hustler consisted solely of the rudder and the two elevons; the latter combined the functions of elevators for controlling pitch and the ailerons for controlling roll.

Convair B-58A-20-CF, serial number 61-2080, the final Hustler completed, is preserved at the Pima Air & Space Museum, Tucson, Arizona. This aircraft was completed and accepted on October 26, 1962, and served with the 305th Bombardment Wing.

Red covers are installed on the engine inlets of B-58A-20-CF, serial number 61-2080. The covers kept out foreign objects and also protected the inlet spikes.

The B-58A at the Pima Air & Space Museum is fitted with a two-component pod, seen here from the front right.

The B-58A is observed from the aft right quarter, showing details of the tail stinger, the fire-control radome, and the dorsal fin and rudder.

The tail stinger and vertical tail are observed from below, showing the concentric, tapering rings that make up the flexible part of the stinger.

The underside of the Hustler at the Pima Air & Space Museum is viewed. The light-colored panels in the foreground are covers for the Doppler radar receiver and transmitter antennas. Farther forward are bomb pylons (two per side) and the two-component pod.

In another view of the underside of B-58A-20-CF, serial number 61-2080, the two-component pod is to the left, the right main landing-gear bay is to the right, and the forward left bomb pylon is between them.

The camera lens and perspective make the two-component pod seem smaller than it actually is in reference to the bottom of the Hustler airframe. In the foreground is the kicker of the TCP, aft of which are four louvered vents in the bottom of the fuselage.

Convair B-58A-20-CF, serial number 61-2059, nicknamed "Greased Lightning," is on static display at the Strategic Aerospace Museum, Offutt Air Force Base, Bellevue, Nebraska. The aircraft was previously displayed at the Octave Chanute Aerospace Museum, where these photos were taken, until that museum's closure. The plane was assigned to the 305th Bombardment Wing, and, in Operation Greased Lightning on October 16, 1963, the plane, piloted by Maj. Sidney J. Kubesch, flew nonstop the 8,028 miles from Tokyo to London. The flight took 8 hours, 35 minutes, and 20.4 seconds and required five in-flight refuelings.

The nose shock strut of "Greased Lightning" is viewed looking downward, showing the two forward arms of the nose landing gear to the sides. The pilot could steer the nose-gear wheels, and the wheels returned to center when the retraction process began.

The nose landing gear is seen from the right side, showing the truss design of the forward arms, which, with two similar, upper arms, supported the shock strut. The bottom of the right upper arm, which terminates in a round bearing, is visible below the landing-gear-bay door.

Both of the main landing gears are visible from under the right wing. The wheels and tires were very small for the size of the plane and were subject to occasional mishaps throughout the B-58's operational career.

"Cowtown Hustler," B-58A-15-CF, serial number 49-2458, was the aircraft whose crew won the Bendix Trophy in 1962. Housed today at the National Museum of the United States Air Force, where this photo was taken, it is today the best-preserved B-58 existent. The operational life of the B-58 was relatively short, lasting for a decade, but the aircraft pioneered many new technological advances, and the plane was an important part of the US strategic arsenal during the height of the Cold War. *National Museum of the United States Air Force*